10/96

WONDERS OF THE WORLD

GALÁPAGOS ISLANDS

Jean F. Blashfield

Technical Consultant

Carrol L. Henderson
Minnesota Nongame Wildlife Biologist
Gálapagos Islands Tour Leader
and
Primary Photographer

RSVP
RAINTREE
STECK-VAUGHN
PUBLISHERS
The Steck-Vaughn Company

Austin, Texas

A production of B&B Publishing, Inc.

Editor – Jean B. Black
Photo Editor – Margie Benson
Computer Specialist – Dave Conant
Interior Design – Scott Davis

Raintree Steck-Vaughn Publishing Staff

Project Editor – Helene Resky
Project Manager – Joyce Spicer

LIBRARY OF CONGRESS CATALOGING-IN-PUBLICATION DATA

Blashfield, Jean F.
    Galapagos islands / Jean F. Blashfield
        p. cm. — (Wonders of the world)
    Includes bibliographical references and index.
    ISBN 0-8114-6362-1
    1. Natural history — Galapagos Islands — Juvenile literature.
2. Galapagos Islands — Juvenile literature. 3. Wildlife
conservation — Galapagos Islands — Juvenile literature.
[1. Galapagos Islands. 2. Natural history — Galapagos Islands.]
I. Title. II. Series.
QH198.G3B58 1995   94-3030
508.866'5 — dc2   CIP
                                                          AC

Cover photo	Title page photo	Table of Contents page photo
Sea lions and Sally Lightfoot crabs on the rocky shore of James Island	**A giant tortoise from Floreana Island**	**Galápagos penguins on a rocky cliff of Bartholomew Island**

PHOTO SOURCES

Cover Photo: © Carl von Wodtke

Courtesy Department Library Service, American
    Museum of Natural History, Neg. No. 326697:
    46

Courtesy Department Library Services, American
    Museum of Natural History, Neg. No. 327355:
    45

J.D. Griggs/U.S. Geological Survey: 11, 15 right

Carrol L. Henderson: 1, 3, 5, 6, 7, 8, 9, 10, 12, 13,
    14, 15 left, 21 all, 22, 23 both, 25 both, 25, 26,
    27 both, 28 both, 29 all, 30, 31, 32, 33, 34, 35,
    36, 37 both, 38 both, 39 both, 40 both, 41, 42
    all, 43 top, 44 both, 48, 50, 52, 53, 54, 55 both,
    56, 57, 58 both, 59, 61

Bill Roberson, Inca Floats: 20

© Susan Speck: 43 bottom, 60

Lisa Turner: 4

© Wes Walker: 18

Printed and bound in the United States of America.
    1 2 3 4 5 6 7 8 9 10 VH 99 98 97 96 95 94

Table of Contents

Chapter One

Distant Islands

Inca kings, English pirates, a Spanish bishop, Charles Darwin, Herman Melville, volcanoes that still rumble, cormorants that can't fly, penguins thousands of miles from the South Pole, dancing boobies with blue feet, lizards that dine in the sea, and the biggest tortoises on Earth—all have at least one thing in common. Each plays a part in the story of one of the most unusual groups of islands in the world's oceans.

Out in the Pacific Ocean, 600 miles (966 km) from the South American continent, right on the equator, lies a chain of islands pushed up from the beneath the sea. Sometimes called the Enchanted Isles, they are more often known as the Galápagos Islands for their most famous residents, giant tortoises, called *galápagos* in Spanish.

The islands are officially owned by the nation of Ecuador. After the name *Insulae de los Galópegos* was used on a map in 1570, the islands were called by that name. However, in 1892, Ecuador decided to honor Christopher Columbus by calling them Archipiélago de Colón, meaning "Columbus's archipelago" (a chain of islands). But the island group is never called by that name except on official documents.

The group of islands consists of 19 dots of land large enough to be called islands, plus perhaps 40 other small rocks and islets. Only a few of the islands are inhabited by human beings. Each one has its own unique wildlife, and each one is equally astounding to naturalists.

The total land area of the archipelago is only 3,086 square miles (7,993 sq km), spread out in an area of sea covering 23,000 square miles (59,570 sq km). The largest island, Isabela, takes up more than half the land area. And the highest point in the archipelago is on Isabela. It is Wolf Volcano, 5,600 feet (1,707 m) high.

There are not many places on Earth that have played such a small role in human history as the Galápagos. This is primarily because there is only one source of fresh water in the islands—not enough to support many people. There are no signs that prehistoric humans ever lived there.

Some of the islets in the Galápagos Islands are more like large chunks of rock in the water. They don't even show up on maps.

Few of the islands can be approached by a large boat. Tourists must visit most islands by small craft. These visitors are on Bartholomew (right).

Discovery

When the Spanish invaders from Europe first conquered the Inca civilization in South America in the 1500s, Spanish historians recorded all the local history they could persuade the storytellers to relate. One story told of Tupac Yupanqui, an Inca prince. Around 1485, he sent an expedition westward from Cuzco, the capital of the Inca Empire (now in Peru). Instead of disappearing into the sea, as some people feared might happen, the adventurers came back with tales of an "island of fire."

The island the travelers found may have been one of the volcanic Galápagos Islands erupting fresh flows of lava. However, they also brought back some black slaves and a brass throne. The Galápagos certainly had no black natives and no source of brass. Perhaps the explorers landed farther north on the South American coast, but nobody can really be sure.

The first verified discovery of the archipelago by Europeans occurred in 1535, when Tomás de Berlanga, the Bishop of Panama, was sent on a mission to mediate between two factions of soldiers fighting in Peru. He sailed southward from Panama, expecting to reach Peru. But when the winds died, an ocean current flowing westward from the continent took control of his ship, carrying it far from the mainland.

Central America

EQUATOR

Galápagos Islands

South America

The Galápagos Islands are isolated in the Pacific Ocean, 600 miles (966 km) from the coast of South America.

The lava chunks forming a small circle called the Devil's Crown near the island of Floreana are still so rough that they appear to have recently flowed out of a volcano.

The sailors feared that they were going to disappear forever into the vast sea and die of thirst in the process. But after about a week, they caught sight of some low, dark islands lying on the horizon. They landed, but they failed to locate a freshwater source for several more days. The bishop and his sailors were more interested in water than in wildlife, but they saw enough to write down descriptions of the giant tortoises. Thirty-five years later, the bishop's notes gave a cartographer the idea of calling the islands Galápagos.

A Nice Place to Visit, But . . .

Sailors of the Pacific seas quickly spread the word about the island chain located west of South America. They even knew that they could stop there and replenish their fresh water (if they hit the right island) and food supplies. But what they didn't know was how to reach the islands when the ocean currents and the winds played tricks on them.

Sometimes the sailors could see the dark and forbidding giant rocks rising from the sea ahead of them, but they often lost their way in the strange mist that formed around the islands. They thought that witchcraft might be moving the islands, always keeping them just out of reach of their ships.

Moreover, some maps of the early 1700s recorded two groups of islands in the vicinity of the Galápagos. Navigation was still an inexact science at the time, and different navigators recorded different latitudes and longitudes for the islands' location. The idea arose that perhaps the islands moved. Thus they came to be called "Las Islas Encantadas," or the Enchanted Isles.

The islands soon became a convenient hideaway for pirates seeking a refuge or a base from which to attack Spanish galleons carrying gold away from the mainland. Through the centuries, treasure hunters have sometimes ventured onto the Galápagos Islands of Floreana and Santiago because of persistent rumors that pirates may have buried treasure on them.

Floreana served for many years as a makeshift international post office. Sailors would leave letters in a barrel on the beach of a certain bay to be picked up by the next passing ship. The sailors on that ship would personally deliver letters addressed to their home countries. Because of this unique tradition, these letters were never mailed with stamps! The bay is still called Post Office Bay.

The barrel in Post Office Bay on the island of Floreana has served as an international mail stop for hundreds of years—and you can still use it today.

New Kinds of Livestock

Once Europeans discovered the Galápagos, humans began to bring changes to the islands where wildlife alone had reigned for so long. Word spread from seaport to seaport about the giant tortoises found there. These ancient creatures had the awesome ability to live for almost a year when stacked on top of each other in the hold of a ship—a year without food, water, or light. The sailors could kill the giant creatures as they were needed for food. It has been estimated that when whaling in the Pacific was at its height in the nineteenth century, thousands of tortoises were taken from the islands.

The tortoises left behind on the islands were just as seriously affected by something else the old-time sailors often did. Because the sailors knew they would be returning to the Galápagos to stock up on tortoises, they sometimes left domestic animals on the islands. They expected the animals to fend for themselves and to breed and multiply before their ships returned. The livestock did indeed multiply. Domestic animals such as cattle, cats, dogs, donkeys, goats, and pigs, as well as the rats and mice that were left on the islands, began to spread out, degrading the habitat of the native wildlife.

The giant tortoises that gave their Spanish name to the Galápagos can live for a hundred years or more.

The Islands No One Could Tame

No one stayed permanently in the Galápagos until 1807, when an Irishman named Patrick Watkins moved onto Floreana. He had an unfortunate habit of waylaying visiting sailors, holding them captive, and forcing them to serve as his slaves. Even with slave labor, however, he gave up in 1809 because of the lack of fresh water. Supposedly he drowned (or ate!) his slaves at sea before showing up on the mainland.

Soon afterward, an American from Louisiana named José Villamil founded a colony on the same island. He and a few fellow colonists brought convicts to work a cattle ranch, planning to sell meat to passing ships. The colonists soon moved to San Cristóbal, which has the only year-round source of fresh water in the archipelago. They left the con-

Pinnacle Rock on the island of Bartholomew stands alone under the hot sun. It has become a symbol of the islands.

victs behind. Both colonists and convicts gradually died, leaving their domesticated animals to multiply and take over the island.

Since the Galápagos Islands were not the tropical islands of people's dreams, no country claimed them until 1832, when, in a rush of nationalism, the newly formed nation of Ecuador decided to claim the islands before another nation did. Even then, Ecuador made little use of them except occasionally to drop off convicts there to survive as best they could. A more permanent prison colony was later built on San Cristóbal. Prisoners were sent to the Galápagos until 1959.

Only three years after the islands were claimed by Ecuador, they were visited just briefly by a young naturalist from England, who was sailing aboard an official survey ship called the HMS *Beagle*. As we'll discover in more detail later, naturalist Charles Darwin

The rough terrain of most of the islands does not welcome human intruders. This blowhole on Hood Island shoots up a stream of water that may reach several stories high.

realized that while the wildlife of the islands was similar to South America's, there were important differences. Understanding the reason for those differences would keep him occupied for the rest of his life. The five weeks that Darwin spent in the Galápagos would ultimately change the world's view of living things.

Attempts to colonize the islands continued over the decades. But the colonists usually gave up because of the isolation and the limited supply of water. However, a few persistent settlers (now called Galapageños) have created farms on some islands.

Today, the island called Santa Cruz is the major center of population. It is also the most frequently visited island because the Charles Darwin Research Station is headquartered there. The population of the entire archipelago is less than 10,000, but more tourists than that visit the island every year. In 1968, Ecuador declared the entire chain of islands Galápagos National Park.

Most of the islands have more than one name. The English, the Spanish, and the settlers have all called them different things. When writer Herman Melville visited the islands in 1841, he observed of the Galápagos, "to them change never comes." But he was wrong. From the day the islands began to appear from beneath the sea, they have known nothing but change.

Chapter Two

Beneath the Enchantment

The Galápagos Islands are quite young by earthly land standards. Darwin realized the land was new when he noted that "the boundaries of most of the lava-streams [were] still distinct."

The older islands of San Cristóbal, Plaza, Baltra, Santa Fé, and part of Santa Cruz emerged from the sea 3 to 5 million years ago. The newer ones, farther west, rose from the sea about one million years ago. That sounds like a long time, but the Hawaiian Islands, which are also volcanic in origin, are at least 70 million years old.

How the Islands Formed

Geologists believe that the Earth's crust is broken up into several different chunks called plates. These plates are always in slight motion, rubbing against each other along a fault line. Occasionally the pressure two plates exert on each other must be relieved. At that time, the plates tremble and earthquakes happen.

Volcanoes continually erupt below the sea. When the lava piles up to above sea level, island groups such as Hawaii and the Galápagos are formed.

Lava cones, such as this one on Bartholomew, are formed when magma (molten rock) breaks through the ground at a spot away from the main volcano vent.

THE GALÁPAGOS ISLANDS

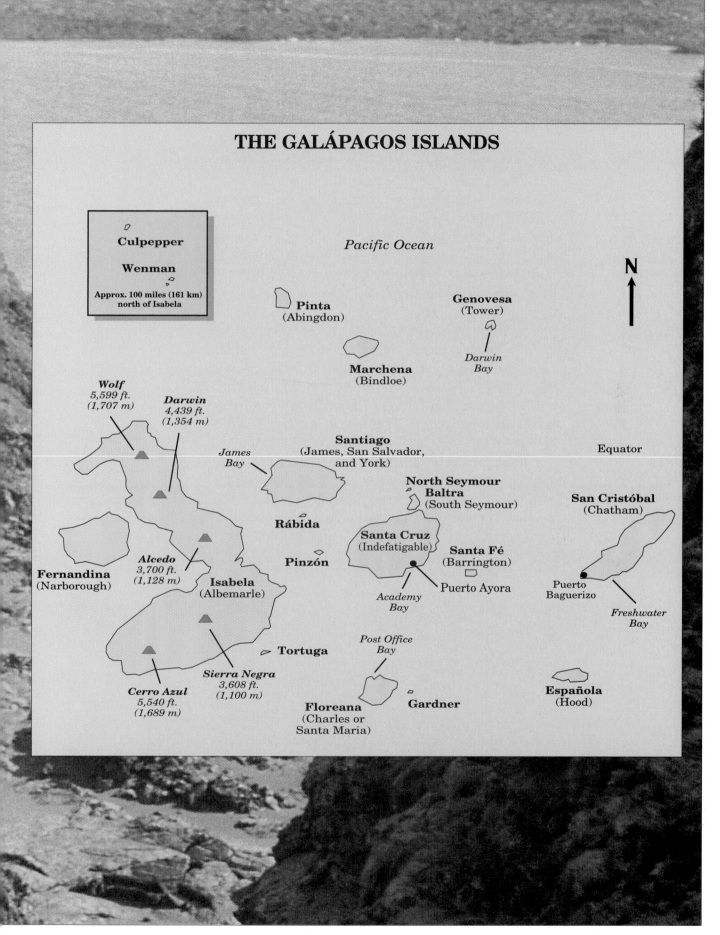

Culpepper

Wenman

Approx. 100 miles (161 km)
north of Isabela

Pacific Ocean

N

Pinta
(Abingdon)

Genovesa
(Tower)

*Darwin
Bay*

Marchena
(Bindloe)

Wolf
*5,599 ft.
(1,707 m)*

Darwin
*4,439 ft.
(1,354 m)*

*James
Bay*

Santiago
(James, San Salvador,
and York)

Equator

**North Seymour
Baltra**
(South Seymour)

San Cristóbal
(Chatham)

Rábida

Santa Cruz
(Indefatigable)

Santa Fé
(Barrington)

Fernandina
(Narborough)

Alcedo
*3,700 ft.
(1,128 m)*

Pinzón

Puerto Ayora

Puerto
Baguerizo

Isabela
(Albemarle)

*Academy
Bay*

*Freshwater
Bay*

*Post Office
Bay*

Tortuga

Sierra Negra
*3,608 ft.
(1,100 m)*

Cerro Azul
*5,540 ft.
(1,689 m)*

Floreana
(Charles or
Santa Maria)

Gardner

Española
(Hood)

When the plates shift to allow the escape of molten lava, volcanoes are formed, and earthquakes occur. However, in places like Hawaii and the Galápagos, there are no fault lines. Instead, the lava from the Earth's core is repeatedly forced up through weak spots in the planet's crust, creating a series of volcanic islands in the middle of a plate. These thin areas on a plate are called "hot spots."

Eruptions of volcanoes that occur on land get a great deal of attention. However, there are many more volcanoes on the bottom of the sea. In fact, there may be as many as 10,000 of them on the floor of the Pacific Ocean alone. Most marine volcanoes erupt for a brief time, form a cone of hardened lava, and then stop. If they erupt long enough, the cone may reach near the surface, where wave action gradually wears it away. Only once in a while do volcanoes continue erupting long enough for lava to build up above the surface of the sea.

The volcanoes forming the Galápagos didn't have to build lava all the way from the ocean floor, which lies an average of almost 3 miles (4.8 km) below the surface. Instead, a big platform of the crust had been pushed up to within about 3,000 feet (915 m) of the surface.

Geologists think that the islands we now call the Galápagos are not the same islands that existed when the islands first started forming. As the plate bearing the volcanoes continued to move across the hot spot toward South America, old islands wore

"Volcanoes created the Galápagos Islands, currents shaped their destiny."

— Richard Hough in *Galápagos—The Enchanted Islands*

Santiago consists of a single volcano that has built up above sea level. Such a large, dome-shaped volcano is called a shield volcano.

This large volcanic rock is used as a resting place by seabirds.

away from wave action and weather, and new ones were formed.

The scientists had no proof of their idea, however, until ocean geologists recently discovered underwater mountains, called seamounts or drowned islands. A large number of seamounts have been located east of the Galápagos. They were volcanic islands that gradually wore away and disappeared under the surface of the sea. The oldest seamount found in the vicinity of the Galápagos so far is at least 10 million years old.

All of the islands in the chain are volcanic in origin, but not all of them are actual volcanoes. Some of them are just chunks of lava that have been heaved up above the surface by earthquakes. Such heaving has not stopped. As recently as 1954, the shore on the western side of the largest island, Isabela, rose 15 feet (4.6 m) quite quickly, just weeks before a nearby volcano, Alcedo, erupted.

Volcanoes and Calderas

Very old volcanic islands, such as Hawaii, have had millions of years for the lava to be eroded into soil in which plants can grow. But the Galápagos Islands are so new that many parts of the islands still resemble giant cinders—hard, blackened remains of ancient fires where almost nothing grows.

Not all the fires are so ancient. Every once in a while, one of the volcanoes erupts, bringing great change to the islands. Some of the volcanoes continue to "boil and bubble" underground, with only occasional puffs of smoke coming out of little holes, called fumeroles, to show that the volcanoes are still active. Isabela and Fernandina, the two most western islands, have seven active volcanoes between them.

When a volcano erupts, a large empty cavern or chamber may be left underground. Sooner or later, the rock above the empty chamber collapses, leaving a crater in the top of the volcano. Such a crater is called a caldera. Some calderas on the Galápagos are up to 6 or 7 miles (9.7 or 11.3 km) wide.

The ground of a caldera can subside, or sink, slowly, over many years. Or, it can fall suddenly. Fernandina, which consists of one huge volcano, used to have a pleasant lake—home to many flamingoes—2,000 feet (610 m) below the crater rim. But in June 1968, the summit of the volcano collapsed very quickly. A giant cloud, almost resembling a nuclear explosion, burst into the sky. Gray ash several feet

Many of the Galápagos Islands still have active volcanoes. The lava cools slowly, forming black cinders.

deep settled over the landscape. The vibrations of the crash were recorded on earthquake instruments around the world, and even sailors on ships far at sea could hear it.

The bottom of the caldera is 1,200 feet (366 m) lower than it was. The lake has formed again in the bottom, and it has shifted location. However, the water in it is not fresh; it's very salty with minerals from within the volcano.

But That's Not Like the Equator!

The Galápagos Islands are located right on the equator. Our impression of things equatorial is that they should be tropical in nature, with palm trees, lush greenery, heavy rains, intense heat, insects, and high humidity. The Galápagos do indeed have such tropical attributes, but only in a few places.

The Galápagos are not typically equatorial land because they are not located in a typical tropical setting. The island chain is washed by two major currents. The Humboldt, or Peru, Current sweeps northward along the west coast of South America. It carries with it the cold temperatures of the Antarctic. When the shallow layer of cold water reaches the vicinity of the Galápagos, it turns westward, joining the warmer Equatorial Counter Current.

During most years, the Humboldt Current keeps the ocean water surrounding the islands as much as 15 to 20 degrees Fahrenheit (8 to 11° C) cooler than nearby waters. These ocean temperatures average

The tall candelabra cactus and shorter opuntia cactus are cacti species found in the Galápagos. This type of plant life is very different from vegetation usually found near the equator.

The lava cactus thrives on volcanic rock, surviving in the hot sun at the equator. It is usually one of the first plants to take root on new lava after it cools. It will begin the process of breaking down the lava to form soil.

WATER TEMPERATURES IN THE GALÁPAGOS

Water temperature differences cause four different zones in the archipelago. These differences are created by the water currents that flow into the region and turn westward past the islands. The most northern islands, including Genovesa, are tropical, and the water is warm. The coldest water is in the western zone, which extends north and south from Isabela and includes part of Fernandina. The southern islands are in a warm sea, and the central islands are in a sea of moderate temperatures.

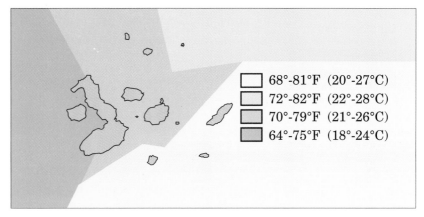

68°-81°F (20°-27°C)
72°-82°F (22°-28°C)
70°-79°F (21°-26°C)
64°-75°F (18°-24°C)

between 64 and 79 degrees Fahrenheit (18 to 26° C). In contrast, Hawaii's warmer ocean water averages between 72 and 80 degrees Fahrenheit (22 to 27° C).

The temperature variations give the islands four different ocean environments within the archipelago. Even a modern traveler on a luxury boat will experience the air temperature dropping ten or more degrees in a few minutes and then rising again an hour or so later as the ship sails on. And the ocean life varies accordingly. The changes in ocean temperatures cause different climates on land, making it possible for a traveler to enter several different zones on one day.

These climate zones determine which animals and plants live where in the archipelago. The cold current allows some animal life of colder regions to survive at the equator. The Galápagos penguin, whose ancestors came from Antarctica, and the Galápagos fur seal, with ancestors from the Chilean coast, are among the cold-loving animals. Joining them on the beaches may be tropic-loving flamingoes. The cold current also causes a great deal of microscopic ocean life to rise from the bottom of the sea. This upwelling makes the region west of Ecuador and Peru one of the great fishing grounds of the world.

The water around the Galápagos is too cool for coral reefs to form easily, but some coral grows around the warm fringes of the islands. These tiny shelled animals are eventually crushed by the surf. Over the centuries, the worn coral skeletons have formed brilliant white beaches on some of the islands. Other islands have black beaches, where lava has been smashed into tiny granules.

The lava gull is appropriately named after the black lava rock that characterizes the beaches and cliffs of many islands in the Galápagos.

The Seasons

Because the Galápagos Islands are on the equator, they don't have a summer or winter as known in more temperate regions. Instead, they have a dry season and a wet season, depending on the ocean currents.

The dry season on the Galápagos is from May or June to December. During this season, the cold ocean current from the south brings cold water to the land. The air just above the water becomes chilled, and moisture condenses out of it in the form of mist, which the natives call *garúa*.

It doesn't seem as if misty, drizzly air should occur during a time called the "dry" season. But the mist doesn't form rain along the low-lying coastal areas. Instead, those areas stay dry and desertlike. However, higher up the mountains something else happens. At an altitude of about 600 feet (180 m), the cold, moist layer meets the warmer air above it. At that altitude, a fine rain falls, creating moist, green, almost junglelike growth. Those islands that are not high enough to reach up to that moisture-laden altitude don't get any rain at all during the dry season.

Toward the end of the year, the winds shift. The warm ocean current coming southward from Central America gets stronger than the cold Humboldt Current. The water around the Galápagos Islands gets warmer,

Isabela is high enough to receive moisture during the dry season. These two tortoises are enjoying a puddle of fresh water on the caldera rim of Alcedo, one of Isabela's volcanoes.

and the air above it also turns warm and starts to rise. The wet season begins.

During the wet season, from about January to May, the air is rain-filled, even on the coasts. At only this time of the year, fresh water is available on all the islands. Unfortunately, the rainy season doesn't last very long, and some years there is no rain at all.

El Niño

During some years, the warm ocean current from Central America is more powerful than usual. Scientists studying old records have found that these extreme times occur every four to ten years. The name *El Niño* is given to these special times because they are usually first noticed about Christmastime, and El Niño means "Christ Child" in Spanish.

A major difference in El Niño years is that the warming of the ocean water extends much farther south than usual. The microscopic life that normally wells up from the bottom of the sea doesn't rise in the warm water, so huge numbers of fish starve to death. That affects the food supply of the seabirds.

Usually, annual rainfall in the Galápagos is less than 3 inches (7.6 cm) on the dry islands and perhaps 40 inches (102 cm) in the wetter regions. However, El Niño can cause these places to get up to ten times more rain than usual. Coastal deserts in South America, about 600 miles (966 km) away, may get heavy rains.

El Niño has a direct effect on the life of the islands. For example, during El Niño of the early 1980s, the supply of sea lettuce (a seaweed) shrank to almost nothing, leaving the marine iguanas nothing to eat. Many of these animals—the only lizards on Earth that feed in the sea—starved to death. On the other hand, the land iguanas dined well on the lush vegetation that the additional rains brought. Two kinds of seabirds called boobies depend on food from along the shorelines. During that El Niño, they failed to breed because there weren't enough fish to feed the existing population, let alone young new birds.

19

Alcedo Volcano is located in the center of the largest island, Isabela. The rim and inside of the caldera are seen here through moss-covered scalesia trees.

THE ISLANDS OF MANY NAMES

Every factor about the Galápagos Islands—location, age, climate, volcanic activity, altitude—gives each individual island a different character. Each has its distinctive scenery, vegetation, and

animals. There are six main islands: Isabela, Floreana, Fernandina, Santiago, Santa Cruz, and San Cristóbal. Fernandina and Santiago are uninhabited. Thirteen smaller islands and over 40 tiny islands called islets complete the archipelago.

Each island has two or more names. The British started naming each of the islands in the Galápagos as soon as they were discovered, and those names are still used in most scientific research because so much of it has been done by the British. However, the Ecuadorians have given the islands official Spanish names. The names used in this book are the names that the residents of the islands tend to use.

Fernandina (Narborough) consists of a single huge volcano about 4,900 feet (1,494 m) high, with a caldera 4 miles (6.4 km) across. In 1968 the floor of the caldera sank an additional 1,200 feet (366 m). This island has the largest population of land iguanas.

Floreana (Charles or Santa Maria) (*above*) is the location of what has been called the world's oldest post office. Patrick Watkins, the islands' first settler, lived here. It later became a prison colony.

Santiago (James, San Salvador, and York) consists of a single volcano. James Bay (*right*) and Buccaneer Bay were the main haunts of pirates.

Isabela (Albemarle) is the largest island. It makes up more than half of the land area of the archipelago. Five of its six volcanoes are still active. The highest, Cerro Azul, is 5,440 feet (1,689 m) tall.

Santa Cruz (Indefatigable), composed of a single large volcano, is the most populated island. It was planted with citrus groves in the mid-nineteenth century.

San Cristóbal (Chatham) is the capital of the islands. Freshwater Bay is located here, where two freshwater waterfalls run off the rough cliffs into the sea. It is the only year-round source of fresh water in the entire archipelago. In the 1860s, a prison colony was established on San Cristóbal. The prisoners provided free labor to large sugarcane plantations which, in turn, provided their food.

The lowest and flattest island is Baltra (South Seymour) (*right*). During World War II, it was a U.S. naval base, charged with protecting the Panama Canal. During the war, the habitat of the unique land iguanas was destroyed, and the animals disappeared. A few survivors were transplanted to North Seymour. The island now has an airport at which most tourists arrive and then take a boat to the other islands.

The smaller, uninhabited islands boast beautiful scenery and magnificent wildlife. Genovesa (Tower) is a "nursery" for breeding colonies of seabirds. Española (Hood) (*below*) is the only known breeding site of the rare Galápagos, or waved, albatross.

The brown pelican swoops over the water and dives for unsuspecting fish, which it catches in its pouchlike beak.

Chapter Three

Castaways and Visitors

Soon after the volcanoes emerged from the sea, living things began to inhabit the Galápagos Islands. Perhaps the wind blowing from the mainland carried a few lichen spores and dropped them on the cooling lava. Lichens are primitive plants—combinations of fungi and algae—that become attached to rock and begin to grow. They began the process of breaking up the solid lava into soil. Gradually, the soil was made even more fertile by the droppings of the seabirds that ventured onto the new islands.

". . . an assortment of windblown, stowaway, castaway, flotsam, and shipwrecked creatures."

— Annie Dillard, in *Teaching a Stone to Talk: Expeditions and Encounters*

Reaching the Islands

Unlike seabirds, lizards could not have reached the Galápagos by flying. But the Galápagos Islands are known for their lizards and other reptiles. So there must have been some other way for larger, nonflying animals to reach the islands. We can never know for certain, but it seems likely that the newcomers arrived on floating rafts of vegetation.

Any time rain falls heavily in the jungles and forests of the South American mainland, some vegetation breaks off and drops into the rivers. Occasionally a clump of tangled tree trunks and grasses accumulates into a floating mat that reaches the sea. These rafts of floating vegetation may contain dozens of rain forest creatures—beetles, frogs, toads, lizards, and snakes. Usually, when the mat reaches the sea, it breaks up, and anything living on it drowns. But perhaps one raft, or two, or three, over thousands of years, was caught by the westward-flowing current and eventually was swept to one of the new islands beyond the horizon.

However, one lone lizard, or one lone mouse, can't begin to populate the islands. By pure chance, though, maybe a male and a female of the same species landed on an island at the same time. The two castaways would then be able to mate, beginning a new population in a new habitat.

Large mammals would probably not survive on a floating raft of vegetation to make the journey to the islands. And, in fact, there are no large land mammals found naturally on the Galápagos.

However they got there, once plants and animals from the mainland reached the islands, they began to adapt, or evolve, into species that were different from their South American cousins. They developed characteristics that helped them survive in the different kinds of living conditions, or habitats, that exist on the different islands. Some of those plants and animals evolved into species unlike any others in the world. They are called endemic species because they can be found only in the Galápagos. For example, 26 of the 57 resident bird species of the Galápagos are endemic. Some of these species occupied more than one island, and ultimately even they became different from each other.

The marine iguanas and land iguanas of the Galápagos are believed to have descended from the common iguana of Central and South America.

The cactus finch is not afraid of the long spines on the opuntia cactus. It ignores them while it eats its meal of cactus seeds.

Island Habitats

The different environments found in the Galápagos are affected by four main conditions. These four conditions are: (1) the ocean currents, (2) the wind direction, which prevails from the southwest, (3) the altitude at which the habitat is found, and (4) precipitation.

The tropics make up just one of the climatic regions on Earth. As you move north or south from the tropics, you reach other kinds of areas—such as subtropical swamps, temperate forests, or deserts—with different kinds of plants and animals. But a visitor to the Galápagos Islands can experience most of those same life zones just by climbing the

This Sally Lightfoot crab lives among the shoreline rocks and tide pools on the island of Santa Cruz.

mountains on some of the islands. Sometimes different life zones are found on different sides of the same island, just because the wind is different.

All the islands, no matter how small, have at least two life zones—shore and arid lowland. The edge of the land, where it meets the sea, is the littoral, or shore, zone. In this sandy zone, living things such as marine iguanas, green turtles, and birds must deal with tides coming in and going out. The main plants are mangrove trees, typical of tropical islands.

Mangrove trees took root in the barren, dry lava of Santa Cruz.

The Arid Lowland

Above the littoral zone is the arid coastal lowland, which extends up to an elevation of about 500 feet (150 m) above sea level. The most common sight in the arid zone is rough lava, where only a few cacti grow, though it may be inhabited by birds and lizards. Only those plants that can establish roots in the little bits of dry soil that accumulate in the cracks of the lava can survive. Brachycereus cacti, for example, have the ability to colonize on fresh lava.

Two different kinds of lava can be found in the desertlike arid zone. One is a smooth, platelike rock called *pahoe-hoe* (pa-HOE-ee-HOE-ee). It was formed when the lava cooled quickly. If the lava of an erupting volcano happened to cool slowly, the rock is all broken up and rough. This lava surface is called *aa-aa* (ah-ah). *Pahoe-hoe* and *aa-aa* are Polynesian words.

In the arid zone, the main vegetation is giant prickly pear cactus. Some of the cacti have been growing for hundreds of years. Boobies nest here, and land iguanas and lava lizards are abundant. Hopping in and out of the scene in this area are different kinds of small brown and black birds called finches. At first glance they look similar, except for some color and size variations. But a closer look shows that different birds have different beak shapes and sizes. We'll learn more about these important birds in Chapter Five.

This *pahoe-hoe* lava found on Santiago formed when the lava cooled quickly.

Island Highlands

Those islands that have high enough mountains (Fernandina, Isabela, Pinta, Santiago, Santa Cruz, Floreana, and San Cristóbal) undergo a complete change in habitat above about 600 feet (180 m). That's where *garúa,* the misty drizzle that occurs during the dry season, condenses into rain. Suddenly, especially on slopes that face the southeast, the growth changes to luxuriant green vegetation. The rain helps break down the lava, creating rich volcanic soil that supports plant life.

Even fairly tall, broad-leaved trees grow here, especially a species called scalesia, which is related to the sunflower. The plants in this family normally do not have woody stems. But in the Galápagos they had no competition to keep them from growing taller and stronger. The tops of the scalesia trees form canopies of green leaves, 35 to 40 feet (9 to 12 m) above the ground, like northern broad-leaved forests. Here in this moist zone called the highlands the famed Galápagos giant tortoises are found.

Most agriculture in the islands is carried out in the green highlands. Bananas and pineapples are among the crops grown for export.

Scalesia trees aren't really trees. They are flowering plants related to sunflowers. But in the Galápagos highlands they grow into huge forests.

The Rest of the Way Up

Above the highlands may be a region often called the "brown zone." A type of guava called *Psidium guajava*, which was brought in by humans, is the main plant here.

At about 1,300 feet (400 m) on the side of the mountains facing south, where it rains a great deal, there is another zone, called Miconia. Miconia is a colorful bush that grows about 6 feet (1.8 m) tall. It is found nowhere else in the world. Ferns grow alongside the Miconia. Only the islands of Santa Cruz and San Cristóbal have a Miconia zone.

Above 1,600 feet (490 m), the tops of the mountains are covered by open grasslands, called pampa. They are moistened by the almost perpetual fog

that hangs over the mountaintops. The zone is tree-less because there is too much wind to allow trees to grow. However, ferns grow abundantly.

Of course, each island is different. Sometimes, the arid zone extends a long way from shore because a mountain blocks the moist winds. That is the case on Santa Cruz. Even each mountain on an island can be different. Only one of the five main volcanoes on Isabela, for example, has a top with pampa.

The rich volcanic soil of the highlands supports lush but low greenery, which provides a home for wildlife.

The Sea Around the Islands

Of course, the region called the Galápagos Islands doesn't stop with the land. The sea around the islands is also part of the Galápagos and its ecosystems.

Like whales, seabirds are free to come and go. They are not endemic to these islands, but several species have chosen to breed in the Galápagos.

Three different kinds of seabirds called boobies live in the islands. They look similar except for the color of their feet: one has blue feet, one red, and one a dirty gray (this one is called the masked booby). They all have sharp beaks that they use to catch fish underwater.

The booby dives from the air, per-haps a distance of 50 feet (15 m) or more, hitting the water like a torpedo. Yet the impact doesn't seem to hurt the bird at all. It has a streamlined body that allows it to dive through the water in pursuit of fish. It catches

Masked boobies are usually found on cliffs or hills next to the ocean. They are the largest of all the boobies that nest in the Galápagos.

them in its bill, which has rough edges that keep slippery fish from getting away.

The three kinds of boobies have divided up the Galápagos food resources. The red-footed booby hunts far out over the ocean, rarely coming within sight of land except at breeding time. The masked booby, the largest of the three, feeds closer to the islands, attracted to schools of fish that swarm in the open waters between the volcanic islands.

This red-footed booby is protecting her egg.

The delightful blue-footed booby (its feet really are blue!) is the only one that hunts close to land. It feeds on the fish that swim in the shallows around the fringes of the islands. Sometimes it hunts by skimming the surface of the sea, dipping down in the water, and then continuing effortlessly on its way when emerging from the water. It seems like a comic at heart because its courtship dance involves showing off its beautiful blue feet.

The three different species of boobies also have established different nesting times so that they don't interfere with each other. Genovesa Island has the largest breeding colony of red-footed boobies in the world. They are the only species of boobies that nests in small trees. The other species nest on the ground.

Nursery Islands

Genovesa, at the northeast "corner" of the archipelago, is a safe haven for many nesting seabird colonies. Around Darwin Bay, thousands of storm petrels nest, hiding their eggs and young in crevices formed by cooled lava from the one volcano that makes up the island.

Blue-footed boobies (*right*) have bright blue feet. The male and female blue-footed boobies (*bottom inset*) are doing a courting dance, which appears to involve showing off the feet. This blue-footed booby chick (*middle inset*) hatched in a nesting area on the east side of Genovesa Island.

Frigate birds (also called man-o'-war birds) nest on Genovesa. Many birds have spectacular courtship displays, but the frigate bird's is one of the most startling. The male has a brilliant scarlet pouch on its throat that fills with air, making it look as if it were a scarlet balloon with a black bird glued to it. As the male proudly displays his balloon, he quivers his wings and makes a warbling sound. The sound and the glorious color of the throat pouch attract a female, which has a white chest.

When the female chooses her mate, she lands by the male, and he continues displaying his red pouch, quivering his wings, and singing his love song. The two spend days, even weeks, building their pair bond and then settle down to the task of building a nest of twigs and small branches. The single egg that the female lays is incubated for almost eight weeks. During that time, the parents take turns leaving the nest to feed.

When it has hatched, the almost helpless chick has to be protected from gulls and other predatory seabirds. A young frigate bird grows much more slowly than most birds, and it is a year or more before it can fend for itself. It must learn to fly far out over the ocean for weeks at a time, catching flying fish and resting on the winds. Frigate birds never land on the water to rest, as most seabirds do, because their wing feathers are not waterproof. A chick must be strong and confident before it takes off for distant ocean waters.

The male frigate bird attracts a female by puffing out the bright red pouch in his chest so it looks like a big balloon. This male seems to have found his mate.

The only place in the world that the waved albatross nests is on Española. This bird spends long months flying, spanning great oceans. It can soar for hours without ever flapping its great wings, taking advantage of every bit of lift provided by the wind.

But every two years or so, all its long life, the waved albatross comes back to Española in April to mate and raise its young. The males and females do a bobbing, sideways dance with each other. They alternately raise their beaks to the sky and bow low, beaks pointed to the ground, while they clack the two halves together. After mating, the female lays a single large egg on the barren ground a long way from shore. She makes no nest.

Although the parents of an albatross chick may spend several days at a time feeding at sea, they return to disgorge into the chick a nutritious oil that is digested in the parents' bodies. Within a few weeks, a chick has its full feathers and takes off over the ocean. The chick does not return for at least three years.

Other birds nest only in the Galápagos Islands, such as the Galápagos penguin, a flightless cormorant, and two unusual gulls. However, these birds live year-round in the islands, so they are included in the wildlife discussed in the next chapter.

This red-billed tropic bird swoops low over the ocean. The tail streamers often are longer than the bird's body.

SPERM WHALES OF THE GALÁPAGOS

Sperm whales travel the oceans of the Earth and are often thought to be among the most dangerous animals alive. Writer Herman Melville's fierce white whale, Moby Dick, was a sperm whale. But the 50-foot- (15-m-) long sperm whales that spend time around the Galápagos Islands are, like most of the island's wildlife, gentle and almost tame.

During the late eighteenth century, the British sent expeditions around the globe. One of the discoveries they made was of the sperm whales around the Galápagos. As the news of the great new whaling site was reported, ships began to converge on the islands, led by the New England whalers. During the next decades, the sperm whale population came close to being destroyed.

Finally, around 1850, word went out again: the Galápagos whales are gone! Whalers began to bypass the island group. Fortunately, they were wrong. Enough sperm whales were left for the population to begin to increase, though the whales' numbers have never again approached the numbers that once roamed the planet.

Chapter Four

Wildlife Like Nowhere Else

There seems to be no rhyme nor reason as to which animals succeeded in making homes on the Galápagos Islands and which did not survive. Whatever the reason, it meant that those animals that did thrive met no natural enemies until human visitors brought some in recent centuries.

In modern times, visitors have been awed by the unusual and fascinating animals that are endemic to the islands. Fortunately for the people but unfortunately for the animals, the animals don't run or fly away when humans approach. They are among the tamest "wild" animals known on Earth.

Charles Darwin wrote, "A gun here is almost superfluous." The sailors who visited the islands discovered immediately that they only had to walk near a sea lion or other animal and club it instead of actually going hunting. The giant tortoises could literally be herded on board their ships. Birds may land on a visitor's head. Iguanas barely blink when a human walks by.

The Galápago of Galápagos

Giant tortoises used to inhabit most of the tropical world. These animals that the Spanish called *galápagos* are left over from prehistory. But history has caught up with them. Only in the Galápagos and on little Aldabra Island in the Seychelles of the Indian Ocean do they exist today.

There are few of the really huge tortoises left, but in past centuries they have been known to reach 5 feet (1.5 m) in length and weigh 500 or 600 pounds (227 or 272 kg). How old they would have to be to reach such a size is not certain, but records have been kept on one animal for at least 150 years. Perhaps these remarkable animals reached 200 years of age, or even more, in the past.

The two main types of tortoises live in two very different habitats. The most common tortoises have dome-shaped shells, or carapaces, that are not indented around the short neck. They also have short legs. These characteristics let the tortoises nibble the lush but short vegetation common in the humid, green regions on higher mountains. These tortoises tend to trundle slowly along, looking toward the ground, ignoring the world around them.

In drier areas closer to sea level, the tortoises called saddlebacks have longer necks. The front edge of the shell is notched above the neck, allowing the animal to raise its neck to reach higher

Sea lions seem unconcerned as yet another boatload of tourists explores their island. They would probably allow the tourists to pet them, but the tourists are allowed to only look—not touch.

vegetation, such as the leaves of shrubs and trees. These tortoises can even raise their heavy weight on just three legs in order to reach higher branches and leaves. The saddlebacks are the tortoises that have come closest to being made extinct because they lived lower on the islands, in areas that were easier for visiting sailors to reach.

The island of Fernandina apparently had tortoises at one time. But the only record of one found there was made in 1906, when Rollo Beck, a scientist with the California Academy of Sciences expedition, killed what turned out to be the last remaining tortoise. Perhaps a large eruption had killed the others. If so, this one had lived on alone for a long time, until it became the largest saddleback tortoise ever seen. The scientist couldn't have known that he was killing the last of the subspecies.

Originally there were 15 different subspecies of giant tortoises. At least three of these subspecies are now extinct. Ten of the species lived on ten different islands. The other five lived on one island—Isabela—but each resided in a separate volcanic crater. The separation of the subspecies on Isabela may have occurred thousands of years ago when each volcano was a separate island. Then the whole platform on which the five islands had developed was raised up by the movement of the Earth and resulted in the five mountains connecting and forming one island.

The largest remaining population of giant tortoises lives in the green highlands on the big volca-

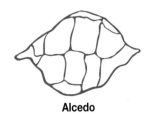

Alcedo

Sierra Negra

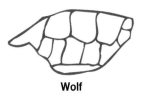

Wolf

The giant tortoises don't chew their food so much as slowly grind it to a pulp. This tortoise lives on the slopes of the Sierra Negra volcano on the island of Isabela.

noes of Isabela, where visitors rarely go. There they spend the hot hours of the day resting in the shade of low trees and coming out to feed on the grasses and shrubs.

There are no rushing streams of sparkling water for the tortoises to drink from, so they depend on the little pools that form in crevices when moisture-laden air condenses on cool rock. Highland rain accumulates into ponds, and flowers bloom within the calderas. That's when the tortoises mate—early in the wet season in the months of January or February.

When ready to nest, the females trudge to the far side of the caldera where conditions are drier. Or,

The plates making up tortoise shells vary from island to island, as can been seen in these five illustrations. Plates even differ between volcanos on a single island.

San Cristóbal

Santiago

some make their way down to the coastal desert. There each one digs a shallow hole and lays two to sixteen round eggs. Then she covers them and leaves. The eggs have hard shells that will keep the developing embryos safe through four to six months, incubated only by the daily warmth of the sun.

Finally, just as a new rainy season is starting, the eggs hatch, and the tiny hatchlings emerge. Animals that may eventually reach 400 or more pounds (181 or more kg) weigh only 3 ounces (93.3 g) when they first hatch. Those that hatch in the caldera spend several years growing in the drier land before joining the other tortoises in the moist areas to the south. Their shells don't harden until they are several years old, leaving them vulnerable to rats, birds of prey, and other predators. They won't mate until they are about 20 years old. Probably not more than one percent of all tortoises that hatch survive their first year.

Because of the long dry season in the islands, giant tortoises have developed an ability to go for months without water. They spend those times almost motionless, perhaps in the shade of a tree, waiting patiently for rain to come back. Once the rains start again, they begin to move, searching for pools of water and a chance to return to a more active life. As new grass grows, they begin to munch their way across the grasslands. At night, they trundle into the nearest pond, where they are protected

This tiny Hood Island tortoise will live at Darwin Station until it is old enough to survive in the wild on its own.

by the warm mud from cold nighttime temperatures and annoying mosquitoes. The tortoises have traveled the same paths for so long that well-worn trails have been cut across the mountainsides.

There were probably once as many as 75,000 giant tortoises on the islands at one time. But as soon as the whaling ships began to come to the area, their numbers started to shrink. Sometimes marauding pirates and sailors killed 400-pound (181-kg) animals to obtain as little as 5 pounds (2.3 kg) of fresh meat. Perhaps more than 200,000 of them were "kidnapped" onto ships to feed many crews of sailors over the 300-year period from 1500 to 1800.

Iguanas and Other Lizards

"Black, dismal-looking heaps of broken lava" was what one sea captain called the strange marine iguanas when he saw them lying around in huge masses in the Galápagos. Charles Darwin called them "disgusting" and "clumsy." These reptiles that feed in the sea are found nowhere else on Earth.

Like a dragon of myth, a marine iguana has a row of spines running down its back. Its round and flattened face features a large mouth that seems perpetually to grin. It uses that mouth to munch the seaweed off rocks exposed at low tide. Its tail, flattened vertically, is used as a paddle to maneuver it through the water. When swimming on the surface, a marine iguana keeps its head above the water while it does the dog paddle. But they're anything but clumsy when they dive as much as 35 feet (11 m) down to graze on deep-water algae called sea lettuce. They can stay beneath the surface for many minutes, sometimes as much as an hour.

Marine iguanas gather in large slumbering clusters on the beaches, often piled so haphazardly that you can't tell where one animal ends and another begins. Occasionally they clamber back into the water to dive for more algae. At night they disappear into holes in the shore's lava rocks and cliffs.

These unusual reptiles actually drink salt water, which would kill many animals. The salt is isolated in special

Marine iguanas are excellent swimmers. They can stay underwater for up to an hour in search of sea lettuce and other seaweed to eat.

"They are perfectly harmless, as much so as any animal I know of, notwithstanding their threatening appearance. They have no teeth, and of course cannot bite very hard. They take their food into their mouths by the assistance of the sharp edge of the upper and under jaw, which shut together one a little within the other, so as to nip grass, or any flowers, berries, or shrubbery, the only food they eat."

— Amasa Delano, a visitor in 1817

The face shapes of the two kinds of iguanas are quite different. The land iguana (*right*) has a pointed face. The darker marine iguana (*below*) has a flatter face and a more distinct row of spines down its back.

glands in their faces, which they empty by sneezing. They appear to be spitting at an approaching enemy because the salt is squirted out in small bursts.

There are seven subspecies of marine iguanas, averaging about 3 feet (0.9 m) in length. Each subspecies has different coloring, depending on what the rock of its native island is like. The most distinctive subspecies is found on Española. It has big splotches of pink and turquoise. In all species, the males acquire a reddish hue when mating time comes in January or February. Then the females dig shallow holes in the black sand above the tide line and deposit one to three eggs each. The eggs have soft shells and are oval in shape. They are incubated by the sun's warmth and protected under the sand for several months, until the hatchlings emerge in May. Those that survive the hungry seabirds begin life without protection from a parent.

The marine iguanas probably evolved from common land iguanas, though the two groups separated at least 15 million years ago. Land iguanas look fiercer than their marine relatives, perhaps because of their more pointed heads. Also, land iguanas are larger—3 to 4 feet (0.9 to 1.2 m) long.

The Galápagos land iguanas are very closely related to the big lizards of South America. Some islands no longer have populations of land iguanas, though they may have had some in the not-too-distant past. On Baltra, American sailors built and maintained an

Three kinds of lizards in one location in the Galápagos: from right to left are a small lava lizard, a marine iguana, and a land iguana.

airfield during World War II, destroying the Baltran subspecies' habitat.

Smaller lizards are also found in the Galápagos Islands. The little, scurrying lava lizards, for example, have developed into seven different species, living on several different islands. The lava lizard on Española is quite large, perhaps twice the size of the others, or about a foot (30 cm) long. These lizards' coloring varies with the location on the island in which they live, though all have black spots. The adult male lava lizards often eat the babies that have recently hatched. Adult males are distinguished by bright rusty-red throat patches.

Birds

The most spectacular birds of the Galápagos are, of course, the seabirds that island-hop their way around the oceans of the world. But there are other birds that live strictly on the Galápagos Islands. They vary from the little, brownish-gray finches to big, beautiful flamingos.

The Galápagos flamingos compose the only population of flamingos known in the Pacific Ocean. They are related to the birds of the West Indies. One recent count placed the number of these tall, rose-colored birds at fewer than 130 specimens. They live in clusters around saltwater lagoons on several islands, where animals introduced by humans damage their

The tiny lava lizard can be found underfoot on most islands. This lava lizard from Española is the biggest of its kind, reaching perhaps one foot (30 cm) in length.

nests. Another problem may be human visitors. It is important for the breeding areas of the flamingos to be protected from disturbance by tourists while nesting is underway.

It can't fly, and it walks clumsily, but the rare flightless cormorant of the Galápagos swims very well. Cormorants are familiar seabirds the world over, but only the large Galápagos species is flightless. Apparently because of the convenience of fish for food and the lack of predators, the cormorants didn't need to fly to survive. Eventually they lost their ability to fly at all. Now it is seriously endangered because it tends to get caught in lobster and fishing nets when it swims. After diving for fish, it walks onto the beach and spreads its wings to dry.

Mockingbirds are the helpful insect-eaters of the Galápagos Islands. All of the large reptiles have a terrible time with insect pests. Mosquitoes and ticks annoy the tortoises, and fleas get into the skin of the land iguanas. But this fact provides the mockingbirds with their meals. All they need to do is land on the back of a passing reptile and dinner is served.

These Galápagos mockingbirds are different from mainland mockingbirds. There are four species of

The yellow-crowned night heron on Española seems to disappear against the rock.

The graceful flamingo has become an endangered species in the Galápagos. This bird belongs to a flock on Santa Cruz.

Galápagos mockingbirds found on most of the major islands. Unlike their relatives in the Americas, the island mockingbirds are predators. In addition to the insects they pluck from other animals, they raid reptile nests and eat baby or wounded birds of other species and hatchling sea turtles.

The Galápagos hawk is another species endemic to the islands, although it is a relative of the red-tailed hawk of North America. The Galápagos hawk is the only bird of prey found flying the daytime skies of the islands. Hawks tend to fly in groups and may even form small flocks around the heads of humans. Farmers have killed off a large part of their population, but the birds have still not learned to shy away from people, even though it would help them survive.

The black-colored adult hawks nest in arid regions on the edges of islands, on rocks, or on low trees. Several males may mate with one female, and all of them will work at nesting and protecting the fluffy hatchlings. These hawks often feed on land iguanas that may be up to 3 feet (0.9 m) long. After killing one, they feed on it until the carcass is light enough to carry back to the nest. The hawks are also scavengers, eating dead fish and crabs.

The swallow-tailed gull is the only gull in the world that fishes at night and the only one that has a forked tail. It probably flies at night to keep its food from being stolen by the ever-present frigate birds. Adults can also remain on the cliff-top nests during the day, keeping their young safe, and then fly out to feed at night. The white spot at the base of the gull's

This species of mockingbird can be found only on Española.

A swallow-tailed gull feeds her chick on Genovesa.

bill appears to help the chicks locate the parent's bill, and the food it contains, in the dark. Being nocturnal, they have larger eyes than other gulls.

One species of penguins has made its way northward along the west coast of South America from Antarctica to the equator. The Galápagos penguin lives primarily on the western shores of the islands farthest west. It stands only about one foot high (30 cm). It swims 3 to 4 feet (0.9 to 1.2 m) underwater in pursuit of small fish. Near Bartholomew Island, the penguins are so tame that they may actually swim among tourists who are snorkeling. There are probably only about a few thousand Galápagos penguins left in the world. They may be in danger of becoming extinct because their distribution is so limited.

Finches

Finches are little, nondescript birds that hop busily around the cacti and rocks. There are large numbers of finches, but they are so common—and so small—that visitors hardly notice them. But, as we'll see in the next chapter, Charles Darwin noticed them and began the thinking that changed the science of biology forever.

The Galápagos finches, usually called Darwin's finches, reach 4 to 8 inches (10.2 to 20.3 cm) long. They are all grayish, brown, or black with short tails and a remarkable variety of beaks.

There are 13 different species, living not on 13 different islands but in different habitats on several different islands. The major difference among them is the shape of their beaks. Some of them live on the ground, and their short, stubby beaks are well suited to eating seeds and insects. Others live in tall cacti or in the trees that occur higher up the mountains. The cactus finch has a long, pointed bill that lets it reach into cactus flowers. Another type has a beak adapted to picking insects from the rough skin of

The Galápagos Islands boast their very own species of penguins—a bird very far from its Antarctic relatives. These shy animals are an endangered species.

iguanas. Tree finches have shorter, thicker bills that let them dig into tree bark for insects.

Perhaps the most remarkable of the tree finches are the two woodpecker finches. They occupy the niche that woodpeckers fill in temperate regions. A northern woodpecker has a long tongue that lets it probe into the holes it makes in the bark. But these finches don't have such a tongue. Instead, they actually use tools—they break off cactus spines or twigs and hold them in their beak to probe within the holes. The woodpecker finch inhabits cacti and trees in the arid zone. The mangrove finch lives in trees along the shore.

The largest finch is called the vegetarian tree finch. It doesn't eat insects. Instead, it dines exclusively on buds, fruits, and some soft seeds. The warbler finch, which has the most slender beak, is an insect-eater. The strongest beak belongs to the cactus finch. It uses its beak to flip rocks much heavier than itself to search for insects.

Mammals

The only land mammals endemic to the Galápagos are two species of bats and seven species of rice rats. Both would have been small enough to arrive in the islands on floating rafts, whereas any larger mammal would probably have drowned before reaching the island. Several of the rats have become extinct, killed

Darwin's sharp-beaked ground finch is found on several islands, but on Wenman Island it has taken on a trait completely different from its relatives. In addition to its usual food of seeds and insects, it has taken to stabbing boobies at the base of their soft growing wing and tail feathers with its sharp, pointed beak. When blood begins to flow, other finches come and feed off the bird's blood. Apparently the damage is not serious enough to harm the boobies. Perhaps the finches on this island could be called "vampire finches."

off by the common European black rat that reached the islands by an easier method—hitching a ride on a sailing ship. Two bigger kinds of mammals—the fur seal and the sea lion—may have arrived in the archipelago by swimming. But when they got there, they adapted to their new world.

Galápagos fur seals were almost wiped out a century ago because of their soft, thick, very marketable fur. Since then, they've made a sizeable comeback, but they aren't nearly as abundant as the Galápagos sea lion. Fur seals are not found on all the islands, and they don't congregate in colonies as the sea lions do. They live along the islands' rocky shores, with the largest populations on Fernandina, Marchena, Pinta, and Isabela.

A new fur seal pup, which cannot yet swim, spends hot days keeping cool in a small shady hole, while its mother swims and dives for food. When the sun goes down, the two get together again. The fur seal mother calls for her pup with a low sound that grows into a high-pitched scream. Each mother's sound is different. When food is scarce—during El Niño, for example—mother fur seals may disappear for several days to feed, leaving the infants to fend for themselves. As a result, many of them die.

The Galápagos sea lions are a subspecies of California sea lions. They are found most often in large, noisy colonies that may contain a thousand animals—with all of them seemingly bellowing, barking, or mewing at once. Santa Fé Island has the largest population of sea lions—about 30 "harems" of 80 sea lions each.

Watchful adults have to keep young sea lions from falling prey to sharks and killer whales in the nearby

Dolphins are sea mammals that live in the Galápagos. They love to play near the tourist boats as the boats travel from island to island. The dolphins dive and weave a few feet in front of the bow of the boat as it breaks through the water.

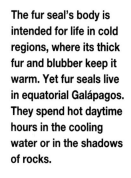

The fur seal's body is intended for life in cold regions, where its thick fur and blubber keep it warm. Yet fur seals live in equatorial Galápagos. They spend hot daytime hours in the cooling water or in the shadows of rocks.

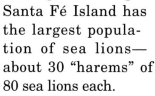

seas. The male sea lion fights so hard guarding his harem that he is usually too busy to eat much.

Eventually he becomes so weak that a stronger bull will come along and take over the harem. The ousted bull may join other males in a "bachelor" colony until he feels ready to try to regain his harem.

Forever curious and playful, sea lions are among the animals that visitors to the islands can easily approach. From only a few feet away it is possible to watch females lie in the sun and nurse their fat little pups. Tourists are not allowed to touch or pet the seals because it could prevent female sea lions from recognizing the scent of their own young. Also, if visitors get too close, male sea lions and females with young can become very aggressive.

Many of the animals endemic to the Galápagos Islands are in danger of extinction. They have no natural defenses against the animals that humans have introduced to the islands. And they have lost the instinctive fear that keeps them away from their biggest enemy—human beings. Humans need to protect the species of the Galápagos from their own generosity!

Bull sea lions constantly compete for harems, spending their time in "bachelor" colonies when they are not "master" of a harem.

A mother sea lion nurses her cub on a shore of volcanic rock.

Chapter Five

Thirty-Five Days that Changed the World

When the British controlled the seas in the nineteenth century, they saw it as part of their duty to map the world in detail, something that had never been done before. Among the ships sent out to do the work of surveying little-known South America was the *Beagle*. It was under the command of Robert FitzRoy. Only 27 years old, he wanted more companionship on the long voyage than would be offered by grizzled, illiterate sailors. FitzRoy sought a young naturalist to accompany him. Although he offered no pay—in fact, the man who went would even have to pay for his own food—it was a wonderful opportunity to study new places for three years or more!

The position was filled by a young student from Cambridge University, 22-year-old Charles Darwin, who described himself as being "extremely fond of geology and indeed all branches of natural history." What he didn't say was that he was capable of recording and thinking about everything he observed in such a way that eventually he turned the basic ideas of biology upside-down. And his visit to the Galápagos Islands started that revolution.

The little ship (the *Beagle* was only 90 feet, or 27 m, long) left England on December 27, 1831. Young Darwin had brought on board all the natural history and geology reference books he could find. He immediately started keeping a detailed journal, one that eventually combined an adventure story with a natural history study. It was published as *The Voyage of the Beagle*.

The journey was originally planned to take

It is difficult to believe that small ships like the *Beagle* once sailed the seas, spending months out of sight of land. By today's standards, sea travel in the 1800s was uncomfortable and dangerous.

three years, but that much time and more passed before the *Beagle* reached the Galápagos Islands. Darwin had already studied the eastern coast of South America. The ship had gone south to Tierra del Fuego, the islands at the southern tip of the continent. There FitzRoy returned three natives of the islands to their homes. On an earlier voyage he had "borrowed" them for several years to show them to the British. Then, mile by mile, the ship traveled up the western coast, giving Darwin numerous opportunities to explore inland for several days— even weeks—at a time.

CHARLES DARWIN

The man who revolutionized biology was born in Shrewsbury, England, on February 12, 1809. He grew up learning to observe the world around him, following the example of his father, a physician, and his grandfather, Erasmus Darwin, an important zoologist. Charles studied first to be a physician and then to be a minister, but he didn't enjoy or do well in either area. While at Cambridge University, however, he developed his lifelong interest in collecting biological specimens. He also became friendly with a number of scientists.

Charles's father was reluctant to let his son accept the position on the *Beagle*, but with his grandfather's help, Charles won approval. No one regretted it.

Until the time of Charles Darwin, biologists accepted the biblical idea that all living things were created at one time—in fact, some were convinced that it happened at 9 A.M. on October 23, 4004 B.C. They also thought that living things were "immutable," meaning that they did not change. Darwin himself went on board the *Beagle* believing that. Even long after, when he was exploring the idea that plant and animal species changed and evolved through a process he called natural selection, he was reluctant to accept his own idea.

After his return to England, Darwin spent several years collecting information on various species and the ways in which they varied. He explored the subject with gardeners, plant breeders, insect specialists, and zookeepers. Finally, in a letter written nine years after his journey to the Galápagos, he wrote: "I am almost convinced (quite contrary to the opinion I started with) that species are not (it is like confessing a murder) immutable." Still he kept delaying publication of his theory.

In 1858, Darwin heard from a naturalist in Malaya who had a theory of evolution very close to his own. He knew the time had finally come to publish his evolutionary ideas. Darwin and the other naturalist, Alfred Russel Wallace, announced their idea jointly at a meeting of the Linnaean Society in London. The following year, Darwin finally published his most famous book, *On the Origin of Species*.

Darwin's theory of evolution began changes in all sciences. Up to that time, most sciences were thought to consist of describing how unchanging things worked. Darwin, however, showed that the whole universe continually changes. Not even the stars are fixed, nor are the species of plants and animals.

After marrying in 1839, Darwin moved his family to Downe, in Kent. Most days he stayed quietly in his study, reading and writing. He had many days when he felt too sick from a chronic illness he picked up in South America to work. Occasionally he traveled up to London to attend meetings of scientific societies. By the time Charles Darwin died in 1882, the Darwinian theory of evolution had been accepted by most scientists the world over.

There were few giant tortoises left on Floreana Island when Darwin arrived.

In the Islands

Darwin's keen eye and recording hand had not yet tired by the time the *Beagle* reached the first Galápagos island, San Cristóbal (which Darwin knew as Chatham), on September 17, 1835. He and his shipmates spent 35 days moving among the islands, climbing their volcanoes, and observing (and collecting) the fascinating and unusual animal and plant life.

Not all of the life on the islands was nonhuman. Darwin found a settlement of 200 prisoners, accused of political crimes and deported from Ecuador to Floreana Island (then called Charles). The prisoners lived inland, up the side of a volcano, at about 1,000 feet (305 m), where the moisture level kept the forests "green as England in the spring time."

The prisoners told Darwin that there were very few giant tortoises left on their island. The domestic pigs and goats that had been released on the island had already multiplied so that they were taking over the wild animals' habitat. It was on Floreana, too, that Darwin realized that nowhere on the islands did palm trees grow, unlike most other tropical islands.

On Santiago (James Island), Darwin camped out for a week while the ship went to find a supply of fresh water. There were Spaniards on the island, catching fish and giant tortoises and then drying the flesh for food supplies to feed the prisoners on Floreana.

Everywhere Darwin went he studied and made notes, but he didn't always understand what he saw. The problem was that, like most scientists of

An oyster catcher, one of the many birds of the Galápagos that Darwin assumed came from South America

Wild animals in the Galápagos today are as friendly and unafraid as their ancestors were when Darwin visited the islands. Because the animals have no instinctive fear of predators, they are extremely vunerable—both to humans and to other animals.

the time, he took it for granted that the islands had once been part of South America. Therefore, if, at first glance, an animal looked like one from South America, he assumed that it was the same species.

This is the way he reacted to the incredible giant tortoises, which seemed to him "antediluvian," meaning "before the biblical flood, or prehistoric." He assumed that they had been brought in from distant places by pirates of old and were unchanged. He accidentally let his specimens of skeletons and shells get mixed up so that he didn't know which islands they came from. However, he didn't think that was important—until he met the governor of the islands and learned from him that each island's tortoises were different from those of other islands.

Darwin located 15 kinds of fish in the sea that he thought might be new to zoologists. He also found 15 new shells, as well as new insects. "It was most striking," he wrote, "to be surrounded by new birds, new reptiles, new shells, new insects, new plants, and yet by innumerable trifling details of structure, and even by the tones of voice and plumage of the birds, to have [South America] vividly brought before my eyes."

Darwin's Finches

The birds that are now called Darwin's finches look very much alike in color and shape, but they have different beaks. These finches probably all descended from a single pair of birds that arrived in the islands millions of years ago from the mainland. Over those years, their descendants have developed different kinds of beaks to adapt to different niches in the environment. They may all be living in the same area and look alike, but they eat different things and don't compete with each other for food or nesting space.

Darwin said of the finches: "One might really fancy that from an original paucity [scarcity] of birds in this archipelago, one species had been taken and modified for different ends." At the time, he was trying to find a logical explanation, but now it is accepted that that is exactly what happened.

Darwin made notes on the birds and even made some sketches of them, as shown at the right. But he didn't draw any conclusions about the birds until later, when he started thinking about the possibility of them evolving from a single source. Nevertheless, he was certain that new species must take a long, long time to develop, which made him wonder if the Galápagos Islands were a lot older than they looked.

Today, biologists are able to explore the natural world in ways that Darwin never imagined. They can study in detail actual chromosomes, the hereditary material of living things. By studying the genes of different species, they can tell how far apart they are in evolution.

Darwin's own drawings of some finch beaks

Biologists have found that 12 of the finch species

NATURAL SELECTION

Writers before Charles Darwin had explored the idea of evolution of plants and animals. Some proposed that a species changed in order to take advantage of something special in its habitat. For example, French biologist Jean-Baptiste de Lamarck suggested that the giraffe had a long neck because generation after generation of the animals kept stretching upward to reach the upper leaves on trees. He thought that the stretched neck could be inherited.

Darwin considered Lamarck's view to be backward. He proposed that the genes in the cells of a living thing could change, or mutate, by chance. If a mutation helped the plant or animal survive and reproduce, the mutated gene would tend to be passed on to the next generation. In the case of the giraffe, those animals born with longer necks had an advantage over shorter-necked giraffes because they had a larger food supply. Over a long time

(nothing happens quickly in evolution!), those animals with longer necks were more likely to be healthy, because they did not have to compete for food, and to produce more offspring. Over thousands, even millions of years, those animals with the long-neck advantage tended to flourish. Those with short necks died out.

To put the idea simply: Lamarck thought that a species took on a characteristic and then changed genetically as a result. Darwin realized that a species changed genetically, allowing it, over many generations, to take advantage of (to "select" for) the characteristic. Darwin thought that by this process, which he called natural selection, one pair of finches, accidentally blown to the Galápagos Islands several million years ago, could gradually evolve into 13 different species that could take advantage of different niches in their island environment.

are so much alike genetically that they could have evolved their different beaks in only a million years, especially because the islands were so isolated. That fits in with what the geologists know about the age of the islands.

However, a genetic study of the two kinds of iguanas—land and marine—shows that they are much farther apart in time. They must have begun to separate as species at least 15 million years ago. Darwin puzzled over the fact that the islands didn't seem old enough for the amount of evolution that had apparently taken place.

The answer has come in recent years, after oceanographers found old islands under the sea's surface, where evolution of one iguana species into two species could have been started. Then, as some islands wore away and disappeared into the sea, the living things could have moved to newer volcanic islands as they rose above the surface and cooled.

It has been theorized that one iguana species evolved into two separate species—land and marine. Land iguanas were almost wiped out on the island of Baltra, but this survivor has been transplanted to North Seymour.

Theory of Evolution

After 35 days in the Galápagos, Darwin accepted the fact that he had to move on, as he had done in so many other places during the previous four years. The *Beagle* headed out on its long passage across the Pacific, toward Tahiti and Australia.

Darwin's small ship returned to England in October 1836, bearing numerous specimens that he had collected over the years. Surrounded by the items he had brought home, his huge volumes of notes, and his memories, Darwin began to work on his book.

But as he worked, his impressions of the giant tortoises, marine iguanas, little brown finches, and other creatures he saw in the Galápagos Islands began to ferment in his brain. By the following spring he was proposing the revolutionary idea that species were "mutable," that they could change.

Biology writer Leonard Engle, in his foreword to an edition of *The Voyage of the Beagle*, summed up Darwin's thought process. "Finally, he saw it plainly: the unusual species of the Galápagos were the descendants of mainland species, reshaped by a new habitat. The isolated Galápagos Islands were a 'laboratory' in which evolutionary processes could be watched at work with a clarity never possible in the confusing babel of species on the mainland."

The sea and the sky together turn Darwin Bay, named for Charles Darwin, into a spectacular sight at sunset. Shown here (*right*) is the harbor at Puerto Ayora on the island of Santa Cruz.

Chapter Six

The Intruders

Hawaii is the only place on Earth that is comparable to the Galápagos Islands. Both chains of islands are far from the continents. Both are volcanic in origin. Both have short human histories (scientists don't know exactly when humans arrived in Hawaii, but they think it was around A.D. 400). Both have plants and animals that developed in isolation. And both are losing their endemic species due to the development of human civilization.

It's too late to rescue much of Hawaii's wildlife. Seventy percent of the endemic species of birds are extinct, and many of the rest are on the endangered list. The plants that appear in Hawaiian tourist brochures are almost all introduced species that have replaced the native ones. But it's not too late for the Galápagos—if people will work to halt the destruction triggered by their own actions.

In 1985, a fire began on the island of Isabela that devastated more than 100,000 acres (40,470 ha) of precious land. Nesting penguins had to flee, leaving their eggs behind. The fire was started by thoughtless people, but humans have been affecting the islands ever since they were discovered by visitors from Western Europe.

Once the word spread across the seas that there were some conveniently located islands out in the Pacific Ocean off the coast of South America, human visitors began to change the islands and their inhabitants. Humans took living things away from the islands and added other living things, changing the islands forever.

Taking Over

There used to be 15 subspecies of Galápagos, or giant, tortoises, but visiting sailors caused the extinction of three, possibly four, of these species. It is estimated that when the sailors started using the islands' tortoises as living grocery stores, there were at least 75,000 animals on the islands. Now they are endangered.

The Brahma cow shown below may look innocent, but as an introduced species, it has helped to endanger the endemic species of the Galápagos Islands.

"As we walked deeper into the tortoise country of Volcan Alcedo, I was saddened to consider the irreversible destruction humans carry with them everywhere. I was embarrassed and ashamed to be one of my own kind. I saw a delicate spider web filled with dew drops and tried to avoid it, feeling that as an alien I did not have the right to demolish it, but I only fell into another I had not noticed. It was hopeless; I was an intruder."

—Tui De Roy Moore, in *Galápagos: Islands Lost in Time*

Sesuvium is an endemic shrublike plant found only in the Galápagos (*right*). Its smooth leaves are adapted to prevent excessive loss of water in the dry climate, similar to a cactus.

Sailors passing through had no idea that dropping goats off—and planning to pick them up later for food—would end up causing great damage to the delicate island ecosystem.

But the collection of the tortoises for food was not entirely to blame for the fact that some of them are now extinct. As soon as the islands became a regular stop on whaling routes, sailors began to leave other animals on them—both accidentally and on purpose. Goats, for example, were left to breed so that other ships could pick them up in later years as fresh food. No thought was given to what the goats would do to the islands.

Most of the islands have had goats for at least two hundred years, and they have come to be a source of food and milk for humans in the islands. But goats do terrible things to the native plants and animals. The way goats eat—nibbling all the way to the roots of a plant—destroys the vegetation. This fact has helped turn major areas of greenery into new, and unwanted, deserts. Where goats live, plant-eating iguanas and tortoises cannot compete for food.

Introducing goats to the islands is not a thing of the past. In 1959, a fisherman put one male and two females on the northern island of Pinta. By 1972, there were an estimated 30,000 goats on the small island, and four plant species had disappeared from the lower elevations.

"The rapidity with which [giant tortoises] are being killed, . . . leaves us but little hope that they will survive any longer than did the American bison after the hide hunters began their work of extermination."

— **Zoologist Rollo Beck in 1906**

In 1971, the Galápagos National Park Service started shooting goats and killed more than 30,000 on Pinta alone during the next five years. The plants recovered and reappeared in their original habitats. Today, there are no more goats on Pinta. Five other islands have been cleared of their goats, but five are still infested.

Pigs are also a problem on the Galápagos Islands. Like goats, they trample and eat the native plants. But unlike goats, they also dig up the eggs of the giant tortoises, green sea turtles, and both land and marine iguanas. The park service is working to eliminate pigs on as many islands as possible.

Over the centuries, visitors sometimes abandoned dogs on some of the islands, and the dogs reverted to wild habits. These feral, or wild, dogs eat not only the iguanas but also fur seals and penguins. They travel in packs and can even be dangerous to humans. Two islands have come close to being wiped clean of iguanas by feral dogs. The dogs are being killed, and iguanas that have been bred and grown in captivity are being reintroduced onto those islands.

Isabela has populations of introduced cattle and horses. Many cows have been exported back to the markets of the mainland—but as a business, not as a means of removing them from the island. Farmers have also introduced the ani, a type of cuckoo from

Goats, since their introduction to the islands, have been nothing but trouble to the native species. To protect the ecosystem, many have been killed. This is one of many goat skulls found lying around.

Dogs abandoned on the islands during the 1800s reverted to the wild. These feral dogs can be dangerous to humans as well as the native mammals.

A CHILD OF THE ISLANDS

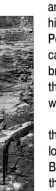

Belgium after World War II was a dreary, lifeless place. The desire to live independently, close to nature, and away from bombed cities sent the parents of little Tui De Roy to the far islands of the Galápagos. Tui spent her earliest childhood in a small clearing among the moist, forested highlands of Santa Cruz. Perhaps twice a year, a ship came from the mainland bringing mail and supplies to the fewer than 400 people who lived on the island.

Seeking more sunshine, the family moved down to the low coastal area at Academy Bay. They brought water to their house in buckets by rowboat from San Cristóbal. Tui and her brother grew up roaming the island and learning about the fascinating wildlife. It was a big adventure for them to sail to one of the other islands to camp out and explore.

As the years passed, the number of residents and visitors increased. Tui watched her archipelago homeland begin to change. Her most cherished activity was taking photographs of her island world, revealing the details that most visitors didn't have time to notice. She investigated where the hardened paths of the giant tortoises went, what happened after a new flow of lava from a volcano, and how life changed during a particularly powerful El Niño.

As she became an adult, Tui De Roy began to publish articles and photographs of the Galápagos in the world's natural history magazines. She revealed insights into the natural world that a mere visitor to the islands could never develop. In 1980, she published a beautiful and fascinating collection of her work in *Galápagos: Islands Lost in Time.* The picture shows some of the unique island wildife Ms. de Roy has photographed—a marine iguana, a yellow-crowned night heron, Sally Lightfoot crabs, and sea lions.

Today, Tui De Roy lives in New Zealand, exploring new worlds. But she attributes to her life in the Galápagos the "capacity to learn through my senses, to understand some of nature's secrets through my feelings, rather than through science and scholarly teachings alone."

Ecuador, which was supposed to pick ticks off of the cattle. Instead, the anis are eating the eggs and young of Darwin's finches.

European black rats were introduced to the islands about a hundred years ago, and since then, they have almost eliminated giant tortoises because the rats eat the soft-shelled hatchlings. They didn't have as much effect on birds because the birds were more protective of their nests. However, four of the seven species of native rats—the Galápagos rice rats—have been exterminated by the intruders. Unlike the larger mammals, it is just about impossible to eliminate black rats from the islands.

Introduced plants can cause problems, too. The guava plant, a nutritious fruit from the mainland of South America, has spread over several of the islands, where it has taken over habitat from native plants. As long as the introduced hoofed animals—cows, goats, and pigs—roam free, they will continue to spread the seeds of the easily grown guava plants. The seeds are passed in the animals' droppings and often land on new sites, where they quickly grow and spread.

Loving the Islands to Death

A major problem with the animals of the Galá-pagos is that they have spent so many millennia without any predators that they don't know enough to be afraid. Even today, when visitors come to the islands by the thousands, the animals are not afraid. For that reason, all tourists must obey strict park rules to minimize the impact of humans on the animals.

Knowing that their animals were special and needed to be protected, Ecuador first declared the Galápagos a wildlife sanctuary in 1934. In 1959, the islands were in the public eye during the 100th anniversary of Charles Darwin's publication of his theory of evolution. Scientists spoke out about their concern for preserving the islands. The government of Ecuador stopped sending prisoners to the islands and declared the uninhabited parts of the islands that nation's first national park. People who had previously owned land there were allowed to keep it, but now only Ecuadorians can move to the islands. However, the local Ecuadorian population is growing at a rate of 10 to 12 percent per year!

In 1979, the islands were named by UNESCO as a World Heritage Site, confirming the belief of many that they are among the most significant natural areas of the world. The entire archipelago was included in the formation of the Galápagos Marine Resources Reserve.

The first cruise ship reached the shores of the Galápagos in 1968. Since then, it has become a popular destination with people who care about wildlife and those who just want an unusual place to visit.

Small ships such as the *Galápagos Adventure,* which can hold 20 people, take tourists from island to island. The number of ships allowed to land each year is limited.

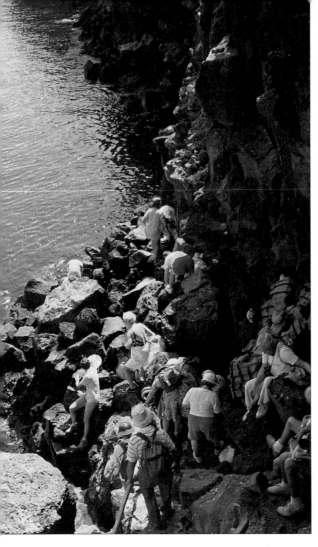

The Ecuadorian government has tried to limit the number of visitors so that about 40,000 people each year come to the islands. The airport on Baltra and the harbors on the main islands have become very busy places.

It would be easy for the government of Ecuador to open the Galápagos Islands to all the tourists who want to go there. After all, lots of money could be earned. But Ecuador recognizes that it has a special responsibility for one of the most unusual natural spots on the Earth. So the government not only limits the number who can visit the islands, but it also restricts where they can go. All tourists arriving in the Galápagos Islands must pay an $80 national park entrance fee to help pay for the park's conservation efforts.

Most "eco-tourists" who arrive care enough about wildlife to be careful and to stick to the marked paths that have been established by the government. All boats must be accompanied by a trained guide. But just the mere fact of many ships and people arriving affects the natural setting. Hikers can wear down the natural trails and smash plants. Ships anchoring in the waters of

Tourists cannot set foot on an island without an official guide. The visitors must stick to clearly marked nature trails and are not allowed to explore on their own. Keeping certain areas of each island off-limits to humans gives the animals a sense of security and territory.

The sea lions in the photo (*below*) are obviously unafraid of humans or their boats.

the islands mean that oil coats the sea, and sewage is dumped into the water. Diesel fuel destroys oyster beds on which many sea animals feed.

While environmentalists focus on the problems created by tourism, long-term pressures are also created by the continuing immigration of native Ecuadorian citizens trying to escape poverty. In 1988, former superintendent of the Galápagos National Park Miguel Cifuentes saw the problems created by this influx of permanent settlers. "Less

A lava tube is the site of an old river of lava that flowed to the sea. Later, more molten lava flowed down over the original, hardened lava river and sealed it inside. After the secondary lava hardened, the original stream broke down and washed away, leaving a cave where the original lava river had been. This is the view from inside a half mile- (km-) long lava tube on Santa Cruz.

than ten years ago people could walk down to the shoreline at low tide and pick up lobsters without even getting wet. Whenever I went to the continent I never thought of locking my house. That has all changed."

Mainlanders move to the islands to make money from the tourists and to work on ranches or carry out farming activities which threaten local ecosystems. Some sell everything they have for a ticket to the Galápagos, not realizing that most of the tourist money goes to travel agencies on the mainland. If there are any jobs on the islands' ranches, the pay is usually very low. So far, the government of Ecuador has been unwilling to set a limit on immigration, however.

Charles Darwin Research Station

Biologists recognize that special care has to be taken to prevent the loss of any more Galápagos species. They have seen what happened in Hawaii as those isolated, volcanic islands developed and became popular.

The Charles Darwin Foundation was established in 1959. UNESCO supported the creation of a headquarters for the foundation, the Darwin Station in the village of Puerto Ayora at Academy Bay on Santa Cruz Island. Scientists could begin to evaluate the natural conditions of the islands and decide what needed doing first.

The main work of the foundation is to provide facilities for scientists visiting from all over the world. In addition, the foundation and the Galápagos National Park Administration have established a program of captive breeding of the endangered giant tortoises. In pens next to the headquarters building, they breed and raise the different species, taking care that they grow up fully. They hope to reintroduce them to the islands from which they came.

Each island had to be analyzed separately and its problems figured out. On Española, for example, the researchers could find only 15 tortoises. The animals lived too far apart to meet for mating and so no new ones were being hatched. The scientists captured all the animals and put them in protective pens. The two remaining males (plus a third loaned

Tortoises are captured and placed in protective pens. Here scientists study and breed them.

by the San Diego Zoo) were able to fertilize the females. The hatchlings grew up protected, and then the young adults were returned to the island. Over 250 tortoises have been moved onto Española where they were almost extinct twenty years ago.

The scientists hope gradually to repopulate all the islands with the appropriate subspecies—if it still exists. When researchers hunted for giant tortoises on Pinta, they found only one old male.

"Lonesome George" is living out his life in captivity, in the hope that a female will be found, but probably the subspecies is extinct.

In the long run, it may not be possible to repopulate all of the islands. On the islands of Pinzón and Española, however, the tortoises that have been returned are now old enough to breed and produce offspring. Since tortoises are so well adapted to live on these islands of scarce water, scientists are hopeful that their conservation efforts will succeed.

In order to have islands that are safe for the tortoises to return to, the Charles Darwin Station has also been responsible for planning and carrying out the extermination of such introduced animals as feral rats, dogs, and pigs that have had such a destructive effect on the native life. Goats have been completely eradicated from some of the islands already. However, conservationists may never be able to finish that unpleasant but necessary task completely because the animals have been in the islands too long and have spread too far.

A Galápagos hawk rests on top of the marker at the entrance to the Galápagos National Park.

A major mission of the Darwin Foundation has been to teach the residents the importance of their natural heritage in the Galápagos Islands. They have come to appreciate that while they are benefiting economically from the visitors, they must help protect the islands.

However, the Darwin Foundation, like Ecuador itself, does not have a lot of money to carry out its hopes for the Galápagos Islands. And, whatever else tourism does, it pays.

With proper management, preservation, and restoration, visitors to the Galápagos will always be able to experience the same delight and awe of discovery known by Charles Darwin. And the many wonderful creatures of the Galápagos can continue to adapt through the processes of natural selection that have made these islands so famous. It will be up to residents, visitors, scientists, and governments of coming decades to see that these unique islands and their unusual wildlife can be preserved.

GLOSSARY

archipelago – a chain of islands.

arid – dry.

caldera – a crater formed when the cone of a volcano collapses.

crust – the outer layer of the Earth, consisting of rock and soil.

El Niño – a periodic warming of the cold Humboldt Current in the Pacific Ocean off South America, occurring when the warm equatorial current dips farther south than usual. The name means "The Christ Child" because the warming generally starts around Christmas time.

endemic – of a plant or animal, found only in one place. Several species of giant tortoises are endemic to the Galápagos Islands.

evolution – the process by which one species of living thing gradually changes into one or more different species through advantageous chance and genetic changes.

fault – the break between two huge blocks of the Earth's crust.

genetic – occurring in the genes, or hereditary material, of a cell.

habitat – the type of place, or setting, where a specific plant or animal lives and thrives.

introduced – of a plant or animal, brought from elsewhere. An introduced animal can take over the habitat of a native, or endemic, species.

lava – foamy, lightweight rock that forms from molten rock from an erupting volcano.

lichen – a primitive, branching plant that is made up of a combination of algae and fungus. Lichens can grow on newly cooled lava.

littoral – existing along a shore.

magma – molten rock inside the Earth. It pours out of a volcano as lava.

molten – in a liquid, or melted, state.

natural selection – Charles Darwin's theory that those individuals with genetic changes that gave them a survival advantage over other individuals would thrive better and reproduce more than those without the genetic changes.

niche – the specific place one species occupies within a habitat. For example, two bird species might share the same habitat, but if one hunts at night and one in the daytime, they have different niches.

species – a type of plant or animal that has common characteristics and will usually reproduce only with its own kind. Darwin proposed the idea that species could change, or evolve, into new species.

subspecies – a type of plant or animal that differs from others of its species, but it could still reproduce within the larger species.

tropical – located in or typical of the region of the Earth near the equator.

FOR MORE INFORMATION

BOOKS
Caruana, Claudia. *Galápagos*. New York: Gallery Books, 1990.
De Roy, Tui and Mark Jones. *Portrait of Galápagos*. Quito, Ecuador: Imprenta Mariscal, 1990.
Harris, Michael. *The Collins Field Guide to the Birds of the Galápagos*. Lexington: Stephen Greene, 1982.
Moore, Tui De Roy. *Galápagos: Islands Lost in Time*. New York: Viking Press, 1980.
Rogers, Barbara Radcliffe. *Galápagos*. New York: Mallard Press, 1990.
Steadman, David W., and Steven Zousmer. *Galápagos: Discovery on Darwin's Islands*. Washington, D.C., and London: Smithsonian Institution, 1988.

VIDEOS
Audubon Video. *Galápagos: My Fragile World*. Photographed by Tui De Roy. Vestron Video.
Mutual of Omaha's Spirit of Adventure. *Beneath the Sea—the Galápagos*. MPI Home Video.
National Geographic Video. *Volcano!* Vestron Video.
Rand McNally Video Expeditions. *Exploring the Galápagos*. International Video Network.

INDEX

Honduras

Honduras

BY SARA LOUISE KRAS

Enchantment of the World
Second Series

Children's Press®

A Division of Scholastic Inc.

NEW YORK TORONTO LONDON AUCKLAND SYDNEY
MEXICO CITY NEW DELHI HONG KONG
DANBURY, CONNECTICUT

Frontispiece: Farmer in the mountains near Paujiles

Consultant: Ricky Abisla, International Observer, Civic Council of Grassroots and
Indigenous Groups of Honduras

Please note: All statistics are as up-to-date as possible at the time of publication.

Book production by Herman Adler Design

Library of Congress Cataloging-in-Publication Data

Kras, Sara Louise.
  Honduras / by Sara Louise Kras.
      p. cm. — (Enchantment of the World. Second series)
  Includes index.
  ISBN-10: 0-516-24871-5
  ISBN-13: 978-0-516-24871-4
  1. Honduras—Juvenile literature. I. Title. II. Series.
  F1503.2.K73 2006
  972.83—dc22   2005024240